Bible Stories
Family Night
Lessons That Teach with Treats

by
Cindy S. Pedersen and Rhea Sidwell

Illustrated by
Val Chadwick Bagley

Covenant Communications, Inc.

For my fantastic, wonderful parents. "The cutest little old couple in the world."

CSP

To my grandkids, the lights of my life: MacKenzie, Lari, Jeni Sage, Nicholas, Lauren, Sara, Kelsi, Hyrum, Jeni, John, and Carolin.

Love, Grandma

Bible Stories Family Night Lessons That Teach with Treats
Cover Design & Illustrations by Val Bagley
Covenant Communications, Inc.
ISBN 1-55503-930-8

Introduction

It's another family night. Your teenager falls asleep during the lesson, and your toddler is bent on destroying your visual aids. Family home evening has become something less than a fun, happy, learning time together. The only time family members seem to be happy with one another and you is when the treats come out.

If any of this sounds familiar, you need this book! It will help you combine those happy times during treats with the learning of exciting scripture stories and gospel principles. Even if your family home evening time is usually peaceful, the lessons and treats provided will help your children remember the scripture stories and their messages even better.

Here's how to use this book:

1. Pick a Bible story that you'd like to teach, or use the lessons in the order they appear in this book.

2. Turn to the corresponding recipe. Collect the ingredients, gather the family together, and have a prayer to start your family night. Begin making the treat, having family members help wherever possible. If you have teenagers, let them take the lead.

3. While you're making the goodies or waiting for them to cook, read the story or tell it in your own words. (Parents may wish to adapt the story depending on the ages of the children involved.)

4. Now, discuss the scripture story to make it stick in the childrens' minds. Discussion questions are provided to help children remember the details of the story, and to understand how they can apply what they've learned to their lives. These aids help children make sense of why they need to read the scriptures.

5. Share your own experiences relating to the scripture story, or have your children share an experience. Take time to talk about your experiences and answer questions.

6. Have fun together as a family while you're learning and eating! Even if the recipes don't turn out exactly right, let your children have fun and experiment.

We hope you enjoy this book and find it useful in your quest to have quality, fun, delicious family time while teaching wonderful scripture stories to your children. Remember, your family will learn better when you TEACH WITH TREATS!

TABLE OF CONTENTS

The Creation Cake

God created a beautiful place for us to live. Children are reminded of this when they see blue gelatin for the water, cake for the land, animal cookies and assorted candies for the plants and sun. Humans participate by eating it all up!

STORY: Genesis 1-3. God created the heaven and the earth. On the first day, God made the light, saw that it was good, then made the darkness. He called the light day, and the darkness night.

On the second day, God divided the waters from the firmament, and called the firmament Heaven.

The third day, God made the dry land appear and he called it earth. He also gathered the waters and called them seas. On the earth, God said that there should be grass and trees and plants, and it was so.

On the fourth day, God made the lights in the sky, the sun for the day, and the moon and stars for the night.

On the fifth day, God put whales and fish in the water and birds to fly in the sky.

The sixth day, God made all the other animals, such as cows, lions, and horses.

Then God said that they should make man in their image. So God created the first man on the earth and named him Adam. He was put in a beautiful place called the Garden of Eden.

God told Adam that he could eat the fruit of any tree in the garden, except the tree of knowledge of good and evil, for if he did, he would die.

God then caused Adam to sleep, and as he did, God made a woman and named her Eve. She was Adam's wife. God commanded them to take care of the garden and to have children.

God looked at all they had made and saw that it was good. On the seventh day, he rested.

DISCUSSION QUESTIONS
1. Who created the earth?
2. How long did it take?
3. What was created each day?
4. What did God name the man and the woman he created?
5. What did God do on the seventh day?
6. What do we do on the seventh day of our week?
7. How can we show our gratitude for all that God has created for us?

RECIPE
White cake mix and ingredients
1 small (3 oz.) package blue gelatin
1 cup boiling water
1/2 cup cold water
3 1/2 cups frozen whipped topping, thawed
Tree: colorful gumdrops with miniature candy bar for trunk
Sun: yellow jelly beans
Animals: animal cookies
Birds: cut a 2" length of a red or black licorice lace. Place in "sky" like a V.
Fishes: use a few gummy or swedish fish and put them in one animal's mouth.

Mix cake mix and ingredients. Pour into greased and floured 13"x9" pan. Bake as directed. Cool in pan for 15 minutes. Make holes in cake every 1/2 inch, using large fork. Pour gelatin into bowl and add 1 cup boiling water. Stir with rubber scraper until gelatin is completely dissolved, about 2 minutes. Add 1/2 cup cold water. Stir. With measuring cup, scoop gelatin out of bowl and pour it over cake. Put cake into refrigerator to chill, about 3-4 hours.

Take pan out of refrigerator. Pour about 1 inch of warm water in sink. Dip just bottom of pan into warm water for 10 seconds. Put large tray upside down on top of cake. Holding tightly, turn tray and pan over, so pan is on top and tray is on bottom. Remove pan.

Frost top and sides of cake with whipped topping. "Draw" a picture with the candies of some of the things created for us: a tree, the sun, animals, etc. Have fun with it! The blue gelatin stripes in the cake represent the water.

Garden of Eden Pizza Bake

The Garden of Eden was a beautiful, blessed place that grew many fruits naturally. You and your family can enjoy some of these fruits on this delicious fruit pizza.

STORY: Genesis 2, 3. Adam and Eve lived in the Garden of Eden, which was very beautiful. Adam named the many animals in the garden. There was plenty of food for them to eat, and God had said that they could eat the fruit of any tree but the tree of knowledge of good and evil. If they ate the fruit of this tree, they would die.

Satan was in the garden, and tempted Eve to eat the fruit of the forbidden tree. Eve said that she shouldn't, or she would die, but Satan said that she wouldn't die, but would know good from evil. He tempted her, saying that the fruit was very delicious. Eve gave in to temptation and tried the fruit. She then gave Adam some of the fruit, and he tried it too.

Soon, they heard God's voice and hid, for they realized that they were naked. The fruit had opened their eyes.

God called to Adam and Eve, and when they came out, he asked if they had eaten the fruit of good and evil. Adam said that Eve had given him the fruit to eat. Eve said that Satan had tempted her, and she admitted to eating it.

God cursed Satan for tempting Adam and Eve. He made coats of skins for Adam and Eve so they wouldn't be naked, then he told Adam and Eve that they would have to leave the Garden of Eden and work for their food. Because they chose to disobey, Adam and Eve were no longer innocent.

DISCUSSION QUESTIONS
1. What was the name of the garden Adam and Eve lived in?
2. God told Adam and Eve they could eat the fruit of any tree but one. Which tree was it?
3. What would happen if they ate the fruit from this tree?
4. Who came into the garden and tempted Eve to eat the fruit? What happened?
5. What happened to Adam and Eve because they had chosen to disobey God?
6. Are there some things God has commanded us not to do? Name some of them.
7. What happens when we disobey God?

RECIPE
1 20-oz. pkg. refrigerated sugar cookie dough or your favorite sugar cookie recipe
1 8-oz. pkg. cream cheese, softened
1/3 cup sugar
1/2 tsp. vanilla
Assorted fruit: bananas, strawberries, kiwi, grapes, etc.

Freeze cookie dough for 1 hour. Slice into 1/8" slices. Line foil-lined 14" pizza pan with slices, overlapping edges slightly. Or roll out your own cookie dough. Bake at 375° for 12 minutes or until golden brown. Cool. Invert onto serving plate; carefully remove foil. Turn right side up.

Combine cream cheese, sugar and vanilla, mixing until well blended. Spread over crust. Arrange fruit over cream cheese layer.

If desired, you may pour a glaze over fruit. Glaze is made by combining: 1/2 cup orange marmalade or peach or apricot preserves and 2 TBSP. water. Heat in small saucepan just until warm.

Eve's Pudding

This story helps to explain why people in the Old Testament burned sacrifices. The dessert takes a while to make, unlike the Garden of Eden Pizza, for once Adam and Eve left the garden, they had to work hard to provide for their family.

STORY: Genesis 3-5. When Adam and Eve left the Garden of Eden, they knew the difference between good and evil. Because of this, they were sometimes happy and sometimes sad. It wasn't easy to raise food and live in the world compared to the ease of their life in the Garden of Eden. But Adam and Eve tried to obey God from then on, and they had many children.

God then commanded Adam and Eve to worship him and to sacrifice the first of their flocks as an offering to the Lord. Adam obeyed, though he didn't know why he was required to do this.

After many days, an angel came to Adam and explained that sacrificing the first of their flocks was like what God would do for them someday when Jesus would sacrifice his life for us. He told Adam that from then on they should repent of their sins, and if they did, they would see God again. Adam and Eve were happy with this news.

DISCUSSION QUESTIONS
1. Why were Adam and Eve sometimes happy and sometimes sad?
2. What are some of the commandments God gave to Adam and Eve?
3. How did Adam make a sacrifice?
4. What did the sacrifice represent?
5. What kinds of sacrifices do we make now?
6. Are you grateful for the sacrifice Jesus made for us? Why? What does it mean?

RECIPE
6 tart apples
6 beaten eggs
4 cups soft bread crumbs
2/3 cup sugar
2/3 cup raisins
1/4 tsp. salt

1/8 tsp. ground nutmeg
Lemon sauce

Peel, core, and finely chop apples. Combine apples, eggs, bread crumbs, sugar, raisins, salt, and nutmeg. Turn into greased and floured 6-cup mold (not a ring mold); cover with foil and tie with string. Place mold on rack in deep pan or in colander inside pan above 1 inch of boiling water. Cover pan and steam for 3 hours. Remove from pan. Let stand 15 minutes. Unmold. Serve warm lemon sauce over warm pudding. Makes 6-8 servings.

LEMON SAUCE: In a small saucepan, melt 2 TBSP. butter; remove from heat. Stir in 1/2 cup sugar and 4 tsp. cornstarch; add 1 cup water and 1 TBSP. lemon juice all at once. Cook and stir until thickened and bubbly.

Abel's Ice Cream Sheep

Abel raised sheep and gave the best of his flock as a sacrifice to God. Because God accepted Abel's sacrifice, and not his brother Cain's, Cain grew jealous. Satan then could work on Cain; he told him to do something really wicked, and Cain obeyed. The sheep you make with your family will help you remember to always give your best to God.

STORY: Genesis 4. The first sons that Adam and Eve had were named Cain and Abel. Abel was a shepherd and Cain worked in the fields.

One day, Abel brought the first and best of his sheep as a sacrifice to God. God was pleased with Abel and accepted his sacrifice.

Cain brought some of his grain to sacrifice, but he did not bring the best and first of his field, so God would not accept it.

One day Cain and Abel were in the fields, and Satan told Cain to kill his brother, Abel. Cain obeyed Satan and killed Abel.

Soon, God came and asked Cain where Abel was. Cain said, "Am I my brother's keeper? Though Cain denied it, God knew what he had done to his brother. God told Cain he would be cursed and driven out of his land.

So Cain and his wife went to live in another place, and life was hard for them.

DISCUSSION QUESTIONS
1. What were two of Adam's sons named?
2. Which one was righteous?
3. Which one loved Satan more than God?
4. Why did Cain kill Abel?

5. What happened after Cain killed his brother?
6. If we disobey God's commandments, can we live with him again?

RECIPE
1/2 cup shredded coconut
2 tsp. chocolate sprinkles
1 pint chocolate ice cream
8 chocolate chips
Lace licorice, cut into small pieces
8 chocolate or black licorice pieces

Put the coconut and sprinkles in a square baking pan, 8x8x2". Mix together. With an ice cream scoop, make 4 balls of ice cream (try to make them as round as possible). Next, make 4 smaller balls of ice cream with a melon ball scoop. Place the balls in the baking pan.

Using 2 spoons, roll the balls around until each one is coated with the coconut mixture. Lift each large ball out of the pan with the spoons and into a dessert dish. Put a toothpick into the top and to one side and place the smaller scoop of ice cream there. Add 2 chocolate chips for eyes and a piece of licorice for the mouth and black licorice for two ears. Put the dishes in the freezer for 10 minutes so the ice cream can get hard again.

Heavenly Cake of Enoch

Enoch and the people of the city Zion were very righteous and obeyed God's commandments. Because of this, they were taken up into heaven. Angel Food cake is very light, the way you feel when you repent of a sin. Do you think you and your family are living well enough to be raised into heaven?

STORY: Genesis 5:22-24; Moses 6:26-68, 7. Enoch was a good man. One day when he was traveling in the land, he heard the Lord's voice from heaven say that he needed to go and prophesy to the people. He needed to tell them to repent, for they were wicked and did not obey the commandments.

When Enoch heard this, he fell upon the ground and said that he was just a lad, and the people hated him because he couldn't speak very well.

But the Lord told Enoch to go and do what he had commanded him to do, for he would be with Enoch and help him say the things he needed to say. God then told Enoch to wash his eyes with clay, and when Enoch did as he was asked, he saw the spirit world.

Enoch then went and taught in many places, telling the people what God had said and that they should repent. Many who heard Enoch were afraid, for he spoke with great power, and they knew God was with him.

Some of the people who listened became righteous, repented, and were baptized. Enoch led the righteous people and built a city named Zion where they lived.

Enoch then had a vision and saw many things that would happen. He saw Zion go to heaven, and he saw Noah and his family being saved.

Enoch saw Jesus Christ die on the cross in his vision, then come back in the last days. He saw that the righteous would be blessed and the wicked would suffer.

God came to visit the city of Zion and its righteous people

9

many times, then he took Enoch and all of the people of Zion into heaven.

DISCUSSION QUESTIONS
1. Who was Enoch?
2. What did God bless him with as he spoke to the people?
3. What did Enoch tell the people?
4. Did any of them believe him? What did they do?
5. What was the name of the city Enoch built? Who lived there?
6. What did Enoch see in his vision?
7. What happened to the city of Zion?
8. Are you living righteously enough right now to be taken to heaven? (Don't answer out loud.)
9. What can we do, as a family, to make our home more like the city of Zion? Let's work on these things during the coming week.

RECIPE
1 angel food or chiffon cake
1 large can prepared lemon pie filling
1 carton (4 1/2 ounces) frozen whipped topping, thawed
2 2/3 cups flaked coconut

Place the cake on serving plate. Slice the cake into two halves and put the lemon filling on the bottom half. Replace the top. Frost the cake with the whipped topping, using spatula. Sprinkle the cake with coconut. Refrigerate until serving time.

Noah's Ark Cupcakes

Noah obeyed God and built an ark, even though he didn't live near any water. People made fun of him, but he continued obeying God. The animals also obeyed God, coming to Noah two by two to have a place in the ark. Because they obeyed, they were saved when the flood came.

STORY: Genesis 6-8. God saw that all the people on the earth were getting to be very wicked, except for Noah and his family. God told Noah that he was going to destroy the wicked people with a flood.

He told Noah to build an ark of gopher wood and told him just how big to make it. He then told Noah that two of every living thing, male and female, should come into the ark. Noah obeyed God, and the animals were gathered into the ark.

When it began to rain, Noah, his wife, and family entered the ark, joining the animals. It continued to rain for forty days and forty nights. The wicked people were killed in the flood, but Noah and his family were saved, for they had obeyed God and were safe in the ark.

Finally, the rain stopped and the water stayed on the earth for a long time. As the water went down, the ark landed on a high mountain and the land became dry again.

Noah sent a dove out, and when it came back with an olive leaf in its beak, Noah knew the water  had gone down. He and his family and the animals came off the ark and built an altar to God. They offered sacrifices in thanks for their safety. God was happy that they did this, and promised that he would never again destroy the earth with a flood. He then put a rainbow in the sky as a symbol of his promise.

DISCUSSION QUESTIONS
1. What did God command Noah to do when he saw that the people were being so wicked?
2. When the wicked people wouldn't obey, what did God say he was going to send to the earth?
3. How were Noah and his family saved?
4. What is the name of the big ship Noah built? Who went in it?
5. How many days and nights did it rain?
6. What happened to the wicked people?
7. What did Noah do after the rain stopped and he left the ark?
8. What does a rainbow mean?

RECIPE
Chocolate cake mix and ingredients to make it
Cupcake liners
1 cup cold milk
1 package (4 serving size) chocolate instant pudding
3 1/2 cups (8 ounce container) frozen whipped topping, thawed
Animal cookies

Mix cake mix; pour into cupcake liners and bake as directed. Let cool 20 minutes. Pour milk into bowl and add pudding mix. Beat with wire whisk until well blended, about 2 minutes. Stir whipped topping into pudding very gently with rubber scraper until mixture is all the same color. Place about a spoonful of this "frosting" on each cupcake and spread around top of cupcake. On each cupcake put a pair of the same animal, like each pair that came into the ark.

Abraham's Rocky Road Mountain

Abraham loved his son Isaac very much, and when God told him he needed to sacrifice Isaac, the road he traveled was "rocky" and difficult indeed.

STORY: Genesis 17, 21, 22. The Lord appeared to Abraham one day and told him many things. He said that Abraham's wife, Sarah, would have a child and his name would be Isaac. When Abraham heard this he laughed, for he and his wife were very old. But God reassured him.

Soon, Sarah became pregnant and gave birth to a baby boy. They named him Isaac. Abraham and Sarah loved Isaac very much.

God wanted to know if Abraham would obey him, so he told Abraham to go and sacrifice Isaac on a mountain. Abraham did not question God, but rose up in the morning, took two young men and Isaac and some wood, and went to the place God had told him about.

The men stayed at the bottom of the mountain while Abraham, carrying a knife, and Isaac, carrying wood, traveled up the mountain. Soon Isaac asked where the lamb was for the sacrifice, but Abraham told him God would provide it.

Abraham built an altar and put wood on it, then tied Isaac to the altar. Abraham raised his knife to sacrifice his son, but an angel came and spoke to Abraham, telling him not to sacrifice Isaac, for he now knew that Abraham loved God enough to sacrifice his only son.

Just then, Abraham saw a ram caught in the bushes, and he went and got the ram and sacrificed it on the altar he had prepared.

God spoke with Abraham once more. He said he would bless Abraham's family because of his obedience to God.

DISCUSSION QUESTIONS
1. What did Abraham and Sarah name their baby boy?
2. Did Abraham love his son?
3. What did God tell Abraham to do?
4. Do you think Abraham was happy about sacrificing his son?
5. What happened just as Abraham was about to sacrifice Isaac?
6. What did Abraham sacrifice instead?
7. Can you think of another father who loved his son very much and who was

willing to sacrifice him for us? (Heavenly Father)

8. How do you feel about that? (Bear your testimony)

RECIPE

1/2 gallon Rocky Road ice cream

Chocolate syrup

Chopped nuts

Marshmallow creme

Chocolate chips

In a large bowl, scoop the ice cream until it is a mountain shape. Decorate with chocolate syrup, nuts, creme, chocolate chips, and whatever other topping you might enjoy. As you're making it with your family, tell the story of Abraham and Isaac, and of Abraham's climb up the rocky road to the top of a mountain to do what the Lord asked him to do.

Get a large spoon and dish desired amounts into serving dishes.

Jacob's Fruit Pottage

Esau was extremely hungry when he saw his brother Jacob's pottage. Though the pottage was very delicious, was it worth sacrificing his birthright blessing for something which only satisfied for a short time?

STORY: Genesis 25:20-34, 27:1-41. Abraham's son, Isaac, grew up and married a woman named Rebekah. They soon learned that Rebekah could not have children, so Isaac prayed to Heavenly Father and Rebekah became pregnant with twins.

The first twin to be born was named Esau. The next to be born, holding on to Esau's heel, was named Jacob. When the boys grew into men, Esau became a hunter, while Jacob liked to stay at home.

One day when Esau came in from hunting, he was very hungry. Jacob had just cooked some pottage and it looked very good to Esau, who asked Jacob for some of it.

Jacob said that Esau could have some pottage if he would sell his birthright blessing to him. In those days, fathers gave their firstborn son an important blessing, which would have gone to Esau. But Esau was so hungry, he said that Jacob could have the birthright blessing. Jacob paid him for it with a bowl of pottage and some bread.

After many years, Isaac became old and called to Esau, asking him to prepare some meat for him, then to come and get his birthright blessing before he died. Esau went to do as he was told. But Rebekah, Esau and Jacob's mother, knew that Esau had sold his blessing. So she sent Jacob in with the meat, and Isaac gave Jacob the birthright blessing.

When Esau came back and learned what had happened, he was very angry and threatened to kill Jacob, so Jacob fled the land.

DISCUSSION QUESTIONS
1. What did Isaac and Rebekah name their twin boys?
2. Which one was the firstborn?
3. Which one was supposed to receive the birthright blessing?
4. What was the price Esau paid one day for a bowl of Jacob's pottage?
5. Was Esau glad he had given the birthright blessing away?
6. Have you ever given away something precious to you—integrity, honesty, morality, etc.—for something which satisfied you for the moment?
7. What can we learn from this story?

RECIPE
1 11-ounce can mandarin orange sections
1 8-ounce can pineapple tidbits
1 cup seedless grapes
2 ripe bananas, sliced
1 8-ounce carton lemon or orange yogurt

Put a colander in a mixing bowl. Empty the orange sections and pineapple into the colander, letting the juices run into the bowl. Throw away the juices. Put the drained fruit into the mixing bowl. Add the grapes and the bananas. Gently stir the yogurt into the fruit. Spoon into serving dishes. Makes 4 servings.

Jacob's Honey Candy

Jacob had to work seven years, then seven more years to be able to marry Rachel. You and your family will also have to work hard to get your dessert, for you will have to pull this candy. After all the effort, though, as Jacob found, the reward will be worth it!

STORY: Genesis 28-32. Isaac told Jacob to go to the land of Padan-aram to stay with Rebekah's brother, Laban. Isaac obeyed and started off on his journey.

One night, the Lord came to Jacob in a dream and told him that he and his family would be very blessed, and that he would have many children and grandchildren. The Lord also blessed Jacob by saying that he would always be with him.

When Jacob awoke, he was very happy. He poured oil on a pillar of rocks and vowed that he would always follow God and that he would give a tenth of all he had back to God.

On his way to his uncle's house, he stopped at a well and met a woman named Rachel, who was caring for her father's sheep. Jacob fell in love with her and went to Laban, her father, to ask permission to marry her.

Jacob said that he would work seven years for Laban if he could marry Rachel. Laban agreed, and Jacob worked hard for seven years.

At the end of the seven years, Jacob expected to marry Rachel, but he was tricked and ended up marrying Leah, Rachel's sister. Jacob was very upset and told Laban that he wanted to marry Rachel. Laban said that he could marry her if he agreed to work another seven years. Jacob agreed and finally was married to Rachel, the one he loved.

DISCUSSION QUESTIONS
1. Why did Jacob leave his home and start for Laban's house?
2. What happened along the way?
3. What did Jacob promise Heavenly Father?
4. What did Heavenly Father promise Jacob?
5. Why did Jacob work so hard for Laban?
6. What was his reward for doing so?

RECIPE
1 cup sugar
1/2 cup honey
1/4 cup cream

Combine ingredients and boil to a soft-crack stage, then pour on buttered plate. When cool enough to barely handle, pull like taffy.

12 Tribes of Israel Cookies and Cream Pie

Jacob and Esau became friends again, forgiving one another. Jacob was blessed greatly with twelve sons, who, along with their families, became known as the twelve tribes of Israel. This pie, lined with twelve cookies for the crust, will help your family remember how many tribes of Israel there are.

STORY: Genesis 33, 49; Exodus 9:7. Jacob decided to return home and reconcile with his brother, Esau, for he didn't want Esau to be angry at him anymore. On the way there, he sent men ahead of him to tell Esau that he was coming. Then he gathered together many animals--goats, sheep, camels and donkeys--and prepared to give them to Esau as presents.

That night, Jacob wrestled with a messenger from God. At the end of the night, the messenger gave Jacob a new name. He re-named him "Israel" and blessed Jacob.

The next day, when Jacob saw Esau coming toward him, he was afraid and bowed himself to the ground. But Esau wasn't angry at Jacob anymore. He ran to meet Jacob and hugged him and kissed him. Together, the brothers cried.

Esau tried to refuse the gifts of animals that Jacob gave him, but Jacob urged him to take them, for he had been very blessed.

Jacob came to the land of Canaan with his wives and twelve sons. They were called the twelve sons of Israel because Jacob's name had been changed by the Lord's messenger. Each of the sons and their families were called a tribe, so Israel's (Jacob's) family became the twelve tribes of Israel and were called Israelites.

DISCUSSION QUESTIONS
1. What happened to Jacob before he met with his brother?
2. What did Jacob do when he saw Esau?
3. How did Esau react to seeing Jacob again?
4. Is it important to forgive? Why?
5. Is there someone in your family that you need to make friends with again?
This week, do some nice things for them and try harder to get along.
6. How many sons did Jacob have?
7. What were they and their families called?

RECIPE
About 20 chocolate sandwich cookies
1 1/2 cups cold milk
1 cup vanilla ice cream, softened
1 package (4 serving size) instant pudding, chocolate flavor
Frozen whipped topping, thawed (for decoration, if you wish)

Place cookies on bottom and 12 around the sides of a 9" pie plate. Pour milk into a bowl. Add ice cream. Beat with wire whisk until well blended. Add pudding mix. Beat with wire whisk until well blended, about 2 minutes. Let pudding stand for 3 minutes. Pour pudding into cookie-lined pie plate. Put pie into refrigerator to chill until set, about 3 hours.

To decorate, spoon whipped topping into zipper-style plastic sandwich bag. Squeeze extra air out of bag; close top tightly. Snip a small corner off bottom of bag with scissors. Squeeze bag gently to make design. Chill until serving time.

Joseph's Popcorn Balls of Many Colors

Jacob's great love for his son, Joseph, caused him to present Joseph with a beautiful coat of many colors. This made his brothers very jealous and angry. Hopefully, your family won't fight over these popcorn balls of many colors, but will join together in the enjoyment of them.

STORY: Genesis 37:2-35. Jacob had many sons, but he loved 17-year-old Joseph the most. To show his affection, Jacob made Joseph a beautiful coat of many colors. This made Joseph's brothers angry, and they hated him.

Joseph had several dreams which made his brothers hate him even more. The dreams said that Joseph would be a ruler over his brothers and that they would bow down to him. They were angry and would not believe him.

The brothers tended their father's sheep. One day, Jacob asked Joseph to go and see if his brothers were well. Joseph obeyed and went to check on his brothers.

The brothers saw Joseph coming, and they started making evil plans to get rid of him. First they wanted to kill him, but Reuben stopped them and said, "Let us not kill him. Instead, he said that they should just throw him into a pit.

When Joseph came near, they grabbed him and took his coat of many colors and threw him into a pit. Just then they saw some Ishmaelites traveling to Egypt, and they decided to sell Joseph as a slave to them for twenty pieces of silver.

The brothers then dipped Joseph's coat in goat's blood and took it to their father. Jacob was very upset, for he thought that Joseph had been killed by a beast.

21

DISCUSSION QUESTIONS
1. Why did Joseph's brothers hate him?
2. What did Jacob give to Joseph?
3. What did Joseph dream that made his brothers even more angry at him?
4. What did Joseph's brothers do to him when he came to find them?
5. What did his brothers tell Jacob?
6. What does being jealous mean?
7. Have you ever been jealous of anybody? What did you do to get over it?

RECIPE
12 cups popped popcorn
1 cup peanuts
3/4 cup multi-colored milk chocolate candies
1/4 cup margarine
1 bag (10 1/2 ounces) mini marshmallows
1 package (4 serving size) gelatin, any colorful flavor

Pour popcorn into a large bowl. Add peanuts and milk chocolate candies. Mix together with spoon. Put margarine and marshmallows in large microwavable bowl. Microwave on high 1 1/2-2 minutes or until marshmallows are puffed. Using pot holders, take bowl out of microwave. Mix together with spoon.

Add gelatin to marshmallow mixture. Stir with spoon until mixture is all the same color. Pour marshmallow mixture over popcorn mixture in a very large bowl. Quickly stir with spoon until marshmallow mixture evenly covers popcorn mixture. Let mixture cool slightly. Grease your hands well with margarine. Shape mixture into balls with your hands. Place balls on waxed paper until completely cool.

King's Dreamy Chocolate, Chocolate Chip Pie

With God's help, Joseph was able to interpret the king of Egypt's dream. Because of this, many people were saved from starvation when a famine came. Here is another example of how important it is for us to listen to the Lord and obey.

STORY: Genesis 37:36, 39, 40, 41. After Joseph was brought to Egypt, he was sold to Potiphar, the captain of the guard of Pharaoh. The Lord blessed Joseph. Potiphar saw that the Lord blessed him and he liked Joseph very much, so he made him overseer of his house and all he had. Because of this, the Lord also blessed Potiphar's house.

Unfortunately, Potiphar's wife also liked Joseph and wanted him to be with her. Many times he refused, but she persisted. One day, when the men of the house were gone, Potiphar's wife tried to kiss Joseph, but he ran away, leaving his coat in her hands. When Potiphar came home, his wife told him lies about Joseph and Potiphar had Joseph put in prison.

The keeper of the prison liked Joseph and put him in charge. While he was there, he met the king's butler and baker. Each of them dreamed a dream one night, and they told Joseph about the dreams. He interpreted the dreams of the servants.

The butler eventually returned to the king's service. After two years, the Pharaoh had a dream and asked many people to try and tell him what it meant, but none could. The butler then remembered Joseph and told the Pharaoh about him, so the king sent for him.

Heavenly Father helped Joseph tell the king what the dream meant. The people of Egypt would have more food than they needed for seven years. After that there would be a famine, and no food would grow for seven years. Joseph said the people needed to prepare and store food for when the famine would come.

The king saw that the Lord was with Joseph, so he made Joseph leader over his whole house and gave him fine clothes and the ring from his own finger. Joseph gathered food during the seven good years and saved it. After seven good years there was a famine, just as Joseph had said, and people came to buy food from Joseph.

DISCUSSION QUESTIONS
1. Who bought Joseph in Egypt?
2. What did Joseph do at Potiphar's house?
3. Did Potiphar's wife like Joseph? What did she do?

4. What lies did she tell Potiphar?
5. What happened to Joseph?
6. How did Joseph get out of prison?
7. Do you think the Pharaoh and the people were happy they listened and obeyed Joseph? Why?
8. What are some things our prophet has told us to do to prepare? Are we ready?

RECIPE
1 1/2 cups cold milk
1 package (4 serving size) chocolate instant pudding
3 1/2 cups whipped topping, thawed
1 packaged chocolate crumb crust
1/2 cup chocolate chips
1/2 cup miniature marshmallows
1 cup chocolate sauce

First make the pudding by pouring milk into large bowl and adding pudding mix. Beat with wire whisk until well blended. Let mixture stand 5 minutes or until slightly thickened.

Fold the whipped topping, chocolate chips, and marshmallows into pudding mixture and spoon into crust.

Freeze pie until firm, about 6 hours or overnight. Remove from freezer. Let stand at room temperature about 10 minutes to soften before serving. Drizzle with chocolate syrup. Makes 8 servings.

Baby Moses' Cake Basket

The king of Egypt was afraid of a "deliverer" being born to free the Israelite slaves, so he ordered that all baby boys be killed. It's ironic that the king's own daughter found the baby Moses in a basket and raised him, and he, with the Lord, did eventually deliver the Israelites.

STORY: Exodus 1-2. Many years after Joseph helped to save the Egyptian people, there was a Pharaoh who didn't like the Israelites. He was afraid that there were too many of them. He feared they would join together against him, so he made them into slaves.

They worked hard and built great cities for the Pharaoh, but the Pharaoh was still worried. He decreed that all the baby boys would be killed.

One Israelite mother had a son and hid him for three months to keep him from being killed. When she couldn't hide him anymore, she put him in a basket of bulrushes and put it in the river, having the baby's sister make sure he would be safe.

That same day, the daughter of Pharaoh came down to bathe at the river and saw the basket. She was curious and sent her maid to get it. When she opened it, she saw the baby. She called him Moses because she drew him out of the water, and he grew up in the Pharaoh's house.

DISCUSSION QUESTIONS
1. What did the king of Egypt do to the Israelite people?
2. Why did he do this?
3. What horrible decree did he send out?

4. What did one Israelite mother do?
5. What did the king's daughter call the baby? Why?
6. What would you have done if you found a baby in the river?

RECIPE
1 pound cake loaf
Any chocolate frosting or frosting from Noah's cupcakes
Licorice stick

Remove cake from wrapper and place on large tray. Frost top and sides of cake with frosting. Curve licorice stick and poke into the cake for basket handle. Put cake into refrigerator to chill until serving time.

Burning Bush Flaming Pudding

Jesus Christ spoke to Moses from a bush that seemed to be on fire, but did not burn up. He speaks to us in a different way now. Are we listening?

STORY: Exodus 2-4. When Moses grew into manhood, he went among the Israelites and saw an Egyptian beating an Israelite. Moses killed the Egyptian and hid him in the sand.

When Pharaoh heard what Moses had done, he tried to have him killed, but Moses ran away to the land of Midian, where he sat by a well. Soon, the seven daughters of the priest of Midian came to draw water for their father's flocks. Just then, some bad men came and tried to scatter the flocks, but Moses helped them.

Jethro, the priest of Midian, took Moses in, and Moses married one of his daughters. One day, Moses was caring for his father-in-law's sheep when he came to the holy mountain. There, he saw a bush that looked to be on fire, but the fire didn't burn the bush. The Lord called to Moses out of the bush and spoke to him. He told him to remove his shoes, for it was holy ground he walked on. He then told Moses who he was and that he had heard the Israelites' cries for help. He told Moses that he should go to Egypt, for the Lord would help him set the Israelites free. Moses said, "Who am I, that I should go unto Pharaoh, and that I should bring forth the children of Israel out of Egypt?"

The Lord assured him that he would be with him. He gave him signs to give the people so that they would know that God had sent him.

Moses was still worried and said that he was "slow of speech and of a slow tongue." But God said that he would teach Moses what to say.

Moses obeyed God and gathered his family together to go to Egypt.

DISCUSSION QUESTIONS
1. What did Moses do when he saw an Egyptian beating an Israelite?
2. Why did he do this?
3. Where did Moses go to get away from the king of Egypt?
4. What did Moses see on the mountain?
5. Who spoke to Moses from the burning bush?
6. What did he tell Moses to do?
7. Has there ever been a time in your life when you were afraid to do something that was right? What did you do? Who did you turn to for help?

RECIPE
2 cups flour
1/3 cup packed brown sugar
1 tsp. baking powder
1/2 tsp. salt
1 tsp. cinnamon
1/4 tsp. nutmeg
1/4 tsp. ground ginger
1/8 tsp. ground cloves
1/3 cup cooking oil
1 cup raisins or chopped dates
1/2 cup chopped nuts
1 cup milk
1/3 cup molasses
4 sugar cubes
2 tsp. lemon extract

In a 2-quart casserole, combine all ingredients and mix until moistened. Cook at 350°, covered, 7 1/2 minutes or until toothpick comes out clean. Let stand, covered, 2 minutes before inverting onto serving plate. Can be served warm or cold. Just before serving, pour 1/2 tsp. lemon extract over each sugar cube and put cubes on top of pudding. Light. When the flames die down, serve with whipped cream.

Heavenly Hail Balls

Through many plagues, including great hail balls, the king of Egypt was informed of the Lord's wishes to have him let the Israelites go. But the king refused to let the people go. What does it take to get us to listen to the Lord?

STORY: Exodus 5-11. Moses went to Egypt as the Lord asked him. He went with his brother, Aaron, to Pharaoh and asked him to let the Israelites go. Pharaoh refused. Moses warned him that if he didn't let the Israelites go, many plagues would come upon him and his people, but Pharaoh would not listen.

Moses said that God would turn the rivers and all the water into blood, and the Lord did. For seven days there was no water, but Pharaoh still would not let the Israelites go.

Next, the Lord made frogs come into the people's houses and in all they had, then lice and flies plagued the Egyptians. After the flies, Pharaoh said he would let the people go, but he lied, for as soon as the flies were gone, he broke his promise.

Moses then warned Pharaoh that the Lord would destroy the cattle, horses, donkeys, camels, oxen, and sheep, but Pharaoh still wouldn't let the people go. Painful boils came upon the Egyptians, then Moses stretched forth his hand and the Lord sent hail and thunder and fire. Any who were outside were hurt badly or killed. Pharaoh came to Moses and said that he would let the people go if he stopped the hail, but again, he broke his promise.

A plague of locusts came next, destroying the fruit and crops. A thick darkness followed. For three days, it was so dark the Egyptians could not even light any lamps or have any light.

After this, the Lord said that every firstborn child would die. The Israelites could have this plague pass over them if they put lamb's blood on their doors. After this night of death, Pharaoh finally agreed to let the Israelites go.

DISCUSSION QUESTIONS
1. Why did Moses and Aaron go to talk with Pharaoh?
2. What did the Lord tell Moses he would do to help convince Pharaoh?
3. What terrible things happened to Pharaoh and the Egyptians because they wouldn't obey God? (There were 10 things.)
4. Did the king of Egypt tell Moses he'd let the people go?

5. What should Pharaoh have done when Moses came to him the first time?
6. Are we listening to our prophet and doing what he instructs us to do, or are we as stubborn as the king of Egypt?
7. What are some things we can work on that the prophet has told us to do? (Examples: food storage, scripture study, family prayer, etc.)

RECIPE
1/3 cup butter, softened
1 package (3 ounces) cream cheese, softened
3/4 cup sugar
1 egg yolk
2 tsp. vanilla or almond extract
2 tsp. orange juice
1 1/4 cups flour
2 tsp. baking powder
1/4 tsp. salt
5 cups flaked coconut, divided

In a large mixing bowl, combine butter, cream cheese, and sugar; beat until mixed. Add egg yolk, vanilla, and orange juice, beating well. Gradually add dry ingredients, flour, baking powder, and salt to butter mixture. Stir in 3 cups of the coconut. Cover tightly and refrigerate 1 hour or until firm enough to handle.

Shape dough into 1" balls; roll in remaining 2 cups coconut. Place on ungreased cookie sheet and bake in a preheated 350° oven for 10-12 minutes or until lightly browned. Let cool about 1 minute, then carefully remove from cookie sheet and cool on wire rack.

Parting the Red Meringue Pie

When Moses parted the Red Sea, the Israelites and Egyptians saw how powerful God really was and how much he wanted the Israelites to escape. With God on their side, they knew that they had nothing to fear.

STORY: Exodus 14, 15. When the Israelites left Egypt, Pharaoh had a change of heart and decided that he didn't want to let the Israelites go, for he had no more slaves to build for him. So he took his army and chased after the Israelites, who had camped by the Red Sea.

Moses' people were afraid when they saw the armies coming. They got angry at Moses for taking them out of Egypt to die in the wilderness. But as the soldiers approached, Moses said, "The Lord shall fight for you and ye shall hold your peace."

The Lord then told Moses to hold up his rod and stretch it over the sea. Moses did as he was told and the water divided, leaving dry land for the Israelites to escape on. To their left and their right there was a wall of water, but it stayed parted until all of the Israelites made it safely across.

The Egyptian army followed after them. The Lord told Moses to stretch his hand over the water. Moses did, and the water that was divided crashed down upon the Egyptian army.

After being saved, the Israelites sang songs to the Lord and celebrated, for they were finally safe and free.

DISCUSSION QUESTIONS
1. Why did Pharaoh take his army and chase the Israelites?
2. Why were the Israelites afraid when they saw the army coming?
3. What did Moses do?
4. How did the Lord save them?
5. What did the Israelites do after they were saved?
6. Have you ever witnessed a miracle? Do you believe they happen?

RECIPE
8" or 9" ready-made graham cracker crust
1 can (21 ounces) cherry pie filling
Red Meringue (below)

Heat pie filling in saucepan over low heat 5 to 10 minutes, stirring occasionally. Remove from heat. While the filling is heating, make red meringue. Heat oven to 400°. Pour the hot pie filling into the pie shell. Spoon the meringue around the edges of the hot pie filling and swirl it with a rubber scraper. Leave an empty spot in the middle for the parting of the red sea of meringue. Bake about 8 minutes or until the peaks of the meringue are a delicate golden brown. Serve warm or cold.

RED MERINGUE
3 egg whites
1/4 tsp. cream of tartar
6 TBSP. sugar
1/2 tsp. vanilla
10 drops red food coloring or more, if needed

Sprinkle the cream of tartar over the egg whites. Beat on high speed until foamy. Gradually beat in the sugar, vanilla, and food color. Continue beating until stiff and glossy, about 5 minutes.

Manna Heavenly Candy

Manna came from heaven in flakes to save the Israelites. Snow also comes down from heaven in flakes. You and your family will enjoy making this unusual candy that you make using snow (or crushed ice).

STORY: Exodus 15:22-27, 16. After the miracle at the Red Sea, Moses took the people into the wilderness. Three days passed and they couldn't find any water. Finally, they came to the waters of Marah, but the water was too bitter to drink. The people got angry with Moses and said, "What shall we drink?"

Moses prayed to the Lord, and he showed Moses a tree which he said to put in the water. Moses obeyed, and the tree made the water sweet so the people had something to drink.

After a time, the people began to murmur against Moses again, for their food had run out and they didn't have anything to eat. But the Lord told Moses he would rain bread from heaven for them.

In the morning, the people found small, round flakes on the ground. Moses said it was the bread that the Lord sent. The people were glad and called it manna. It tasted like wafers made with honey. Each day, the people were told to gather just enough for themselves and their families. Many tried to save extra until the next day, but it would grow worms on it and would stink.

The Lord said that they should only gather extra for themselves on the day before the Sabbath, so they could keep that special day holy. The people did as they were told, and the manna they saved for the next day did not grow worms or stink. The people knew they were being cared for.

The Israelites ate manna for forty years.

DISCUSSION QUESTIONS
1. How did the people react when they found the water unfit to drink?
2. How did the Lord make the water good for the people to drink?
3. When the Israelites ran out of food, how did the Lord save them?
4. What did manna taste like?
5. How much manna were they supposed to pick up off the ground?
6. What happened if they disobeyed and picked up extra?
7. When were they supposed to gather extra?

33

8. Is there "manna" for our spiritual selves that Heavenly Father has given to us and told us to "feast" on each day? What is it? Are we reading the scriptures together as a family each day?

RECIPE
1 cup brown sugar
1/4 cup water
1/2 tsp. vanilla

Boil brown sugar, water, and vanilla until it dissolves. Continue boiling for 2 minutes or until thick and syrupy. While mixture is still hot, take outside and swirl over clean snow. If snow is not available, pour over a large bowl of crushed ice. This makes a chewy, crackly taffy.

The 10 Commanding Layers Parfait

We are greatly blessed to have the Ten Commandments to use as a guide to living a righteous life. Review the commandments and ask yourself if you are truly keeping all of them.

STORY: Exodus 19-21, 24, 31, 34. After traveling in the wilderness for two months, the Israelites came to Mount Sinai. Moses climbed the mountain, and there he spoke with the Lord. He told Moses to remind the people of how much they had been blessed, for they had been led out of Egypt. Moses needed to tell the people to obey God's commandments, and he would bless them.

After going back down the mountain, Moses gathered the people together and told them what the Lord had said. The people said, "All that the Lord hath spoken, we will do."

Moses went back and told the Lord what the people had said. The Lord told Moses to gather the people at the bottom of Mount Sinai, for he was going to speak to them. A cloud of thick smoke came onto the mountain, and the Lord was in it, and there was thunder and lightning. The people were afraid. The mountain shook and then the Lord spoke to the people, giving them the Ten Commandments:

1. Thou shalt have no other gods before me.
2. Thou shalt not make unto thee any graven image.
3. Thou shalt not take the name of the Lord thy God in vain.
4. Remember the sabbath day, to keep it holy.
5. Honor thy father and thy mother.
6. Thou shalt not kill.
7. Thou shalt not commit adultery.
8. Thou shalt not steal.

9. Thou shalt not bear false witness against thy neighbor.
10. Thou shalt not covet.

The people heard the Lord and stepped back, for they were frightened. They wanted the Lord to talk to Moses, then Moses could tell them what the Lord had said, for they thought they would die if they heard God's voice.

Moses went back to Mount Sinai, and the Lord gave other commandments to the people. Moses told the people what the Lord had said, and they built an altar and made sacrifices, and the people promised to obey the commandments.

Then the Lord had Moses, Aaron, Aaron's sons, and seventy elders of Israel come up the mountain. There, they were able to see the Lord.

The Lord told Moses to come higher on the mountain into a cloud. Moses did, and he was there for forty days and forty nights. During that time, the Lord wrote the commandments on stone with his finger, then gave the stone tablets to Moses.

DISCUSSION QUESTIONS
1. What was the mountain the Israelites came to after traveling for two months?
2. What did Moses do there?
3. When the people stood at the bottom of Mount Sinai, what did they hear?
4. Can you name the Ten Commandments?
5. How did the people react to hearing the Lord's voice?
6. How long was Moses gone on Mount Sinai?
7. What did the Lord give him on Mount Sinai?
8. Are you ready to hear the Lord's voice or see him? How do you think you would react if you had been among the Israelites when the Lord gave them the Ten Commandments?

RECIPE
1 package (8 ounces) cream cheese, softened
2 cups cold milk
1 package (4 serving size) instant pudding, vanilla flavor
1 can (21 ounces) cherry pie filling (or banana slices)
1/2 cup vanilla wafer crumbs
2 cups whipped topping

Beat cream cheese with 1/2 the milk at low speed until smooth. Add pudding mix and remaining milk, beating until smooth.

Spoon 1/3 of the pudding mixture evenly into 4 dessert dishes, then sprinkle with wafer crumbs and cover with pie filling and a layer of whipped topping. Repeat. Top with additional wafer crumbs and one cherry. Makes 4 servings.

Sweet Meringue Clouds

The cloud that the Lord placed over the tabernacle let the Israelites know that he was there. When the cloud moved, then, is it any surprise that the Israelites packed up the tabernacle and followed it, settling wherever the cloud settled?

STORY: Exodus 26-40. The Lord told Moses on Mount Sinai that the Israelites needed to build a tabernacle. He told Moses how it was to be built and commanded the Israelites to donate some of their property to build it.

When Moses came down from Mount Sinai, he told the people what the Lord had commanded. The Israelites obeyed and gave gold and silver for the tabernacle, and animal skins for the roof. Women made beautiful cloth for the walls. Then they proceeded to build the tabernacle the way God told them, making it like a tent with a wall of curtains. Inside the wall was a yard with an altar for sacrifices and a small tent building. This building had two rooms, one with a gold altar in it.

In the other room was the ark of the covenant, a big, beautiful box which held the stones with the commandments on them. There was also a lamp which always burned.

Moses blessed the people and the tabernacle. He then blessed Aaron and his sons and gave them the priesthood.

The tabernacle was like a temple. It was a very holy place where the Lord visited and people came to learn about God and do his work. During the day, the Lord put a cloud over the tabernacle. At night, he created a fire to show the Israelites that he was with them.

When the cloud moved away from the tabernacle, the Israelites took the tabernacle down and carried it with them until the cloud settled over it again.

DISCUSSION QUESTIONS
1. Why did the Israelites build a tabernacle?
2. What did it look like?
3. What was the ark of the covenant?
4. What was the tabernacle for?
5. What was above the tabernacle in the day? At night?
6. Why did the Israelites take down the tabernacle and move it?
7. What is a place that we have on the earth now that is like the tabernacle?
8. Do you want to go to the temple? Why?
9. How can you prepare now to go to the temple?

RECIPE
3 egg whites
1/2 tsp. cream of tartar
1/2 tsp. vanilla
6 TBSP. sugar
3/4 cup chocolate chips

Beat egg whites, cream of tartar, and vanilla until frothy. Add sugar, one tablespoon at a time, and beat until stiff peaks form. Fold in chocolate chips. Drop by big spoonfuls onto a greased cookie sheet and cook in a 375° oven 4 minutes or until lightly browned. Serve and eat immediately. Makes 9 meringue clouds.

Joshua's Bubble Ring Wall

God kept his promise to the Israelites by helping them get to the promised land. By obeying his instructions, the Israelites, with Joshua leading the way, were able to knock down the walls of Jericho and capture the city. It won't take a miracle to knock down your bubble ring wall dessert! It will just take a hungry family!

STORY: Joshua 1-6. After Moses died, the Lord picked Joshua to lead the Israelites to the promised land in the land of Canaan. Other people were living there, but the Lord assured them that he would help them to obtain it.

Joshua sent two spies to Jericho, and they stayed with a woman named Rahab. She told the spies that the people of Jericho were already very afraid of the Israelites, for they had heard of the miracle of the parting of the Red Sea. She asked that her family might be saved since she was helping them. They agreed and went back to Joshua and told him all they had learned.

After three days, they came to the river Jordan. Joshua said that the Lord would be with them, and he was, for as the priests who carried the ark of the covenant dipped their feet in the river, the water parted, as with Moses, and the people crossed it on dry ground. When the priests stepped out of the riverbed with the ark, the water flowed again.

When Joshua first saw Jericho, he also saw a man with a sword. The man explained that he was the captain of the Lord's host, an angel. The Lord then told Joshua how he was to capture Jericho, and Joshua told the people.

Joshua then led the people to the city of Jericho, which had high walls around it. He gathered his army and began marching around the walls of Jericho once a day for six days, the priests carrying the ark of the covenant and leading the way. Seven priests blew their ram's horns while the other men didn't make any noise.

On the seventh day, the army marched around the walls of Jericho seven times, then Joshua told the men to shout. They began shouting and the walls of Jericho fell down, exposing the city. The Israelites captured Jericho. Rahab and her family were saved because she had helped the spies. The Lord had given the promised land to the Israelites.

DISCUSSION QUESTIONS
1. Who was chosen to be prophet after Moses?
2. What miracle occurred when the priests carried the ark of the covenant into the Jordan River?
3. How did the people of Jericho think they could keep the Israelites out?
4. What did the Lord tell Joshua to do to capture Jericho?
5. Did it work?
6. Does it seem impossible that this happened, or do you believe it could happen again? Why?
7. God promised the land to Abraham, Isaac and Jacob. Did he keep his promise? How often does he keep his promises?

RECIPE
20 milk chocolate kisses
1/4 cup butter
2 packages (10 each) refrigerated biscuits
1/2 cup sugar
1/2 tsp. cinnamon

Grease ring mold. Melt butter in saucepan over low heat. Separate the biscuits and flatten each biscuit into a 3" circle. Place an unwrapped chocolate kiss in the center of each biscuit. Wrap the biscuit around chocolate, forming a ball. Pinch edges to seal firmly. Repeat with remaining chocolate kisses and biscuits.

Mix the sugar and cinnamon. Dip each ball in the margarine, then roll in the sugar-cinnamon mixture. Arrange the balls in the greased ring mold, forming two layers. Place the balls of dough in the second layer between the balls of dough in the first layer. Bake in a preheated 375° oven for about 20 minutes or until the bubble ring is golden. Put on cooling rack and cool about 1 minute. Turn mold upside down on a plate and remove the ring mold. Cool about 10 minutes. Serve warm and let your family help the wall come a-tumbling down! Serves 10.

Ruth's Popped Wheat Snack Mix

Ruth showed her goodness by taking care of Naomi and going into the fields to gather wheat and barley to make bread. She was rewarded with a good friend and a righteous husband. Gather your wheat as Ruth did, pop it, follow the recipe below, and you'll be rewarded with a delicious snack mix!

STORY: Ruth 1-4. A woman named Naomi, who lived in Bethlehem, was married and had two sons. Because of a famine, there wasn't enough food to eat in Bethlehem, so they went to Moab to find food. While there, Naomi's husband died. Her two sons grew up and married women named Orpah and Ruth.

After several years, both of Naomi's sons died and she decided to return to Bethlehem. Orpah went back to her family, but Ruth begged Naomi to let her stay with her, for she loved Naomi. Naomi finally agreed, and they went to Bethlehem together.

Once there, Ruth went into the fields of Boaz and gathered wheat and barley off the ground after the gleaners had picked it. Boaz saw Ruth and asked about her. He was impressed that Ruth would take care of Naomi, so he had the gleaners purposely drop grain on the ground for her to gather. Ruth took the grain to Naomi and cared for her.

Boaz liked Ruth's kindness, and he married her. Together they had a son named Obed, who was the grandfather of King David.

DISCUSSION QUESTIONS
1. Why did Naomi and her family move to Moab?
2. What happened there?

3. What were her sons' wives named?
4. When Naomi's sons died, what did she tell her daughters-in-law to do?
5. What did they do?
6. How did Ruth help Naomi in Bethlehem?
7. Who was Boaz?
8. Why is this story important? What does it teach us?

RECIPE
Any kind of whole wheat to cover the bottom of a saucepan
1/4 cup butter, melted
4 1/2 tsp. Worcestershire sauce
1 1/4 tsp. seasoned salt
8 cups Chex cereal
1 cup peanuts
1 cup pretzels

Spray the bottom of a saucepan with non-stick spray. Cover just the bottom with wheat. Stir and cook on high until it starts popping. Turn down to medium heat. When all wheat is popped, sprinkle with salt.

Combine butter, Worcestershire sauce, and seasoned salt, mixing well. In a large resealable bag, pour cereals, nuts, pretzels, and popped wheat. Add butter mixture to bag and seal top of bag securely. Shake until all pieces are coated.

Into a large, microwave-safe bowl, pour the contents of the bag. Microwave on high for 5-6 minutes, being sure to stir thoroughly and scrape sides and bottom of bowl every 2 minutes. Spread on paper towels to cool. Enjoy!

To bake in conventional oven, pour the bag mixture into a roasting pan. Bake at 250° for 1 hour, stirring every 15 minutes.

Samuel's Listening Waffle Drops

It took Samuel four times before he realized God was calling to him. How well do you listen? If you listen carefully, you can hear these cookies bake.

STORY: 1 Samuel 1-4. Hanna was a righteous woman. But she was very sad, for she could not have any children. One day, she went to the temple and prayed for a son. She promised that if the Lord would bless her with a son, she would have him serve the Lord all his life. Eli, a judge and priest, heard Hanna and thought she was drunk. But she explained what she was doing, and Eli said that her prayer would be answered.

A short time afterwards, Hanna had a baby boy and she named him Samuel. Hanna sang praises to the Lord because she was so happy. When Samuel was a little older, Hanna took him to Eli, and asked that he teach Samuel to do God's work. Samuel helped Eli and was righteous.

Eli had two sons who were supposed to help in the tabernacle as well. But they didn't help the people. Instead, they did wicked things. Eli was warned by the people that his sons were wicked, but he still let them work in the tabernacle.

One night, as Samuel lay in bed, he heard someone calling his name. He thought it was Eli, who was in the next room, so he ran to Eli. Eli said he had not called Samuel, and told him to go lie down again. Samuel obeyed, but soon he heard his name called again three more times. Each time he ran to Eli, who kept telling him to go back to bed.

Finally, Eli realized that God was calling Samuel. He told the boy to listen, and when God called again, he should say, "Speak, Lord, for thy servant heareth. Samuel did as he was told, and God told Samuel that bad things were going to happen to Eli and his sons, for Eli had let his sons be wicked.

Morning came, and Samuel told Eli what God had said to him. Later, Eli's sons were killed in battle and Eli died when he heard the news of his sons' death.

Samuel grew and God made him the new prophet and judge.

DISCUSSION QUESTIONS
1. What was Samuel's mother's name?
2. When Samuel got a little older, who did Hanna take Samuel to? Why?
3. What happened one night when Samuel was in bed?
4. What did God tell Samuel?
5. What happened to Eli and his sons?
6. What happened to Samuel?
7. Do you think God will allow wicked people to do sacred work? Why?

RECIPE
1/4 cup flour
1/2 cup butter, softened
2/3 cup sugar
2 eggs
1 tsp. vanilla
1/2 tsp. salt
1 1/4 cup cocoa powder
1 tsp. baking powder
1/2 tsp. cinnamon
1/2 cup chopped nuts
Powdered sugar

Beat together butter and sugar until fluffy. Add the eggs and vanilla and beat well. Stir together flour, cocoa, baking powder, salt, and cinnamon; add to creamed mixture. Stir in nuts. Drop by teaspoonsful 2" apart on a preheated waffle iron. Listen as they cook. Bake until done, about 1 minute. Remove to rack to cool. Sift powdered sugar over cookies. Makes about 48.

Can also be cooked in a 350° oven on cookie sheet, 2 inches apart, for about 10 minutes.

For vanilla waffle drops, omit cocoa and cinnamon.

King Saul's Royal Raspberry Cookies

Saul was chosen to be king of Israel by God, and he enjoyed the luxuries royalty brought. But when he chose to disobey God, he lost it all.

STORY: 1 Samuel 7-15. Samuel was the judge and prophet of Israel. When he became old, he chose his sons to be judges. Unfortunately, they weren't good judges, for they took bribes and made bad judgments. The elders told Samuel that the people wanted a king instead of judges. Samuel was upset that they wanted a king, so he prayed to God to know what to do. God told him to do what the people wanted, for they didn't want God to lead them.

Samuel warned the people that a king would take their children for servants, and he would take their fields and a tenth of their animals. But the people still wanted a king to make judgments and to fight their battles.

A big, tall man named Saul came the next day to speak with Samuel. God told Samuel that Saul was the one who would be king, so Samuel anointed Saul with oil to become the king of Israel. Samuel then called the people of Israel together and told them that God had chosen Saul as their king. Many were happy, but some of the people disagreed, for they did not want Saul to be their king.

But Saul was a great leader. He led the Israelites, and they won in battle. Because of this, the people changed their minds and were happy to have Saul as their king.

Saul was a righteous king for many years, following God and telling the people to follow him as well. But one day, Saul was waiting for Samuel to burn sacrifices before he went to battle, for Samuel was the only one who had authority to burn sacrifices. After a time, Saul got impatient waiting for Samuel to come and decided to burn the sacrifices himself. Soon after, Samuel arrived and saw what Saul had done. Samuel was angry, for Saul had disobeyed God. He told

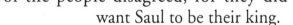

Saul that God would choose another king.

DISCUSSION QUESTIONS
1. Why did the people want a king?
2. What did God tell Samuel to do?
3. Who did God choose to be king?
4. Did the people accept him?
5. How did Saul disobey God?
6. What was his punishment?
7. Are there consequences for the things we decide to do, both good and bad?
8. What if we make a mistake? What should we do to make it right?

RECIPE
1 cup butter, softened
1 1/2 cups firmly packed brown sugar
2 eggs
2 tsp. almond extract
2 cups flour
1 tsp. baking powder
1 tsp. salt
1/2 tsp. baking soda
2 1/2 cups quick oats, uncooked
1 jar (12 ounces) raspberry jam
Granulated sugar for sprinkling

Combine butter and brown sugar in large bowl. Beat until well blended. Add eggs and almond extract, then beat.

Combine flour, baking powder, salt, and baking soda. Mix into creamed mixture at low speed until just blended. Stir in oats with spoon. Cover and refrigerate at least 1 hour.

Roll out dough, half at a time, to about 1/4" thickness on floured surface. Cut out with 2 1/2" round cookie cutter or a round cup. Place 1 teaspoonful of jam in center of half of the rounds. Top with remaining rounds. Press edges with a fork to seal. Prick centers and sprinkle with sugar. Place 1 inch apart on greased cookie sheet.

Bake 12-15 minutes or until lightly browned in a 350° oven. Cool about 2 minutes on cookie sheet, then remove to cooling rack. Makes 2 dozen.

David's Fudgy Stones

With God's help, young David defeated a Philistine giant with only a handful of stones and a slingshot. If the stones gathered had been these delicious fudgy stones, he may not have wanted to throw them at all!

STORY: 1 Samuel 17:1-53. The Israelites fought a battle with the Philistines. One of the Philistines, a giant named Goliath, came forward and taunted the Israelites, daring someone to fight him. He did this for forty days. He said that if someone could kill him in a fight, the Philistines would become the Israelites' servants. But, he said, if he killed the man sent to fight him, the Israelites would become the Philistines' servants.

David was a boy who was an Israelite. He had three older brothers who fought in the battle while he took care of his father's sheep. One day, his father sent David with some food to feed his brothers. There, David heard and saw Goliath. He asked why none would fight him when they had the Lord on their side. But everyone said that they were too afraid.

When Saul, the king, heard what David had said, he sent for him. David told Saul that he would fight Goliath. Saul was amazed. He said, "Thou art not able to go against this Philistine to fight with him: for thou art but a youth, and he a man of war from his youth.

David still wanted to go. He told Saul that he cared for his father's sheep, and he had had to fight and kill a lion and a bear. He said God was with him then, and God would be with him when he went to fight the Philistine.

Saul then agreed and gave David his armor, but David would not wear it to fight. Instead, he chose five stones, took his sling, and went to meet Goliath.

47

When Goliath saw David, he laughed at him and made fun of him because he was so young. But David said to him, "Thou comest to me with a sword, and with a spear, and with a shield: but I come to thee in the name of the Lord of hosts."

Goliath came forward to kill David, and David reached into his bag and took a stone, put it in his sling and let it fly, hitting Goliath in the forehead. Goliath fell to the ground. David then took Goliath's sword and cut off the giant's head.

When the rest of the Philistines saw what had happened, they ran away, for they knew that David had been protected and helped by God.

DISCUSSION QUESTIONS
1. Who was Goliath?
2. Why did he shout at the Israelites? How long did he shout?
3. Who was David?
4. What did David decide to do when he heard Goliath?
5. What did David take with him to fight the giant?
6. What happened?
7. Will God help you if you have a problem and ask him for help, having faith?

RECIPE
9 cups Chex cereal
1 cup chocolate chips
1/2 cup peanut butter
1/4 cup butter
1 tsp. vanilla
1 1/2 cups powdered sugar

Pour cereal into large bowl and set aside. In a 1 quart microwave-safe bowl, combine chocolate chips, peanut butter, and butter. Microwave on high 1-1 1/2 minutes or until smooth, stirring after 1 minute. Stir in vanilla.

Pour chocolate mixture over cereal, stirring until all pieces are evenly coated. Pour cereal mixture into a large sealable bag with powdered sugar. Seal securely and shake until all pieces are well coated. Spread on waxed paper to cool.

For the stovetop method, melt chocolate chips, peanut butter, and butter over low heat until smooth, stirring often. Remove from heat and stir in vanilla. Continue as above.

David And Jonathan's Friendship Cobbler

David and Jonathan's friendship was so great that they covenanted to always look out for one another. Their friendship was tested, but remained true when Jonathan's father tried to kill David. This cobbler has two very different fruits that mix together to create a wonderful new taste. Likewise, David and Jonathan's lives, though different, became entwined for the better.

STORY: 1 Samuel 18, 19, 20. After David killed Goliath, he was brought into King Saul's house. David there met the king's son, Jonathan, and they immediately formed a wonderful friendship. Jonathan loved David so much that he gave him his sword and his clothes, and they made a vow of everlasting friendship.

King Saul became very jealous of David because of his many victories on the battlefield and because all the people loved him. He tried to have David killed by sending him to battle, but David was even more successful. This made Saul even angrier.

Saul told all of his servants, and his son Jonathan, that they should kill David. But Jonathan could do no such thing. He tried get his father to change his mind, but King Saul wouldn't listen.

Jonathan found David and warned him. They worked out a way for David to know if he was still in danger with King Saul. If all was well, Jonathan would shoot three arrows close and tell the boy who helped him that the arrows were close and he should go pick them up. If David was still in danger, he would shoot the arrows far away and tell the boy to go and find them.

Jonathan met with his father that night and learned that he was still intent on killing David. So Jonathan shot the arrows far away and sent the boy after them. David then knew his life was in danger and he had to leave. He said goodbye to Jonathan, and they both cried, for they loved each other.

DISCUSSION QUESTIONS
1. Who was Jonathan?
2. Why did King Saul want to kill David?
3. Did Jonathan let his father kill David? Why?
4. How did David find out that Saul still wanted to kill him?
5. David and Jonathan had a wonderful, lasting friendship. Are you great friends with someone? Have you told them how grateful you are for their friendship?

6. This week, write a letter to your friend, expressing your love and gratitude for them.

RECIPE
1 large can peaches
1 cup raspberries
Yellow cake mix
Whipped topping or vanilla ice cream

Mix peaches (with juice) and raspberries together in a greased casserole dish. Sprinkle cake mix on top and stir a little of the peach juice into the cake mix. Bake at 375° for about 25 minutes or until cake on top is done. Top with whipped topping or ice cream.

Bath-sheba's Beautiful Bombe

When David saw Bath-sheba's beauty, he was tempted and did something he knew to be wrong, for he wanted Bath-sheba for his own. He soon learned that he could not hide his sins from God; eventually, they exploded like a bomb.

STORY: 2 Samuel 11, 12. King Saul saw David defeat Goliath. He knew God had helped him, so he sent for David to come and live in his house. He gave David many things and made him a leader of his army.

The Israelites had a war with the Philistines, and in that war, King Saul and his sons died. David grieved and was very sad.

David then became the next king of Israel. He was a good and righteous king who followed God's commandments.

One night, David walked up on his roof. From the roof he saw a beautiful woman who was washing herself. David asked who the woman was and found out she was the wife of one of his soldiers, a man named Uriah. The woman's name was Bath-sheba.

David wanted her for his wife, but knew he couldn't do that while Uriah was alive, so he sent Uriah to the most dangerous part of the battlefield. There he was killed, and David was free to marry Bath-sheba.

But the Lord knew what David had done. He sent the prophet Nathan to David. Nathan told David that God knew what he had done, for he couldn't keep a secret from God. He prophesied that many bad things would happen to him because of the choice he had made.

David was a king for a long time, and he ruled with righteousness. He wanted his

51

son, Solomon, to be the next king, so he went to Nathan and asked him to anoint Solomon as the next king. He told Solomon to obey God's commandments.

DISCUSSION QUESTIONS
1. What became of David when King Saul died?
2. What did he see one night?
3. What was Bath-sheba's husband's name?
4. What did David do wrong?
5. What did Nathan, the prophet, tell David?
6. Was David sorry for what he had done?
7. Can we hide our sins from God?

RECIPE
2 cans (20 oz. each) pineapple slices, drained
8 maraschino cherries, stemmed and halved
2 1/2 cups cold milk
2 packages (4 serving size) vanilla instant pudding
3 1/2 cups whipped topping, thawed
1 pound cake loaf (12 ounces), cut into 16 slices

Line a 2-quart bowl with plastic wrap and arrange about 16 pineapple slices on the bottom and sides, pushing the slices as closely together as possible. Place a cherry half, cut side up, in the center of each pineapple slice.

Make pudding by putting milk in a bowl, adding the pudding mix, and beating with a wire whisk until well blended. Let it stand 5 minutes, then fold in 1/2 of the whipped topping.

Spread about 1/3 of the pudding mixture over the pineapple. Place about 6 cake slices over the pudding layer and press down gently. Arrange 5 pineapple slices over the cake slices, then layer with 1/3 of the pudding mixture, 4 cake slices, and remaining pineapple. Cover with remaining pudding and top with remaining cake slices. Press down gently. Cover and chill for 1 1/2 hours.

Invert dessert onto serving platter, then carefully remove plastic wrap. Makes 16 servings.

King Solomon Wise Cracks

King Solomon was blessed with great wisdom. Many times when he was judging people, he did some unexpected things to discover the truth. As you and your family crack open your cookies and answer your questions, you can test yourself to see how wise you are.

STORY: 1 Kings 2-3. Before King David died, he told his son Solomon to keep the commandments and follow God. After David died, Solomon became king. He was a very righteous king who followed in God's ways.

God was happy with Solomon and appeared to him one night in a dream. He said, "Ask what I shall give thee." Solomon asked for nothing but an understanding heart to judge the people and discern between good and evil. God was pleased that Solomon didn't ask for riches. He granted Solomon his wish and told him there was never a wiser man before him, nor would there be anyone wiser after him.

When Solomon awoke, he was grateful and burned sacrifices to show his thanks. That same day, there came two women who lived in a house together. The women had babies that were nearly the same age. The first woman said that during the night the other woman's baby died, and that she had exchanged her dead child in the night for this woman's living child. But the other woman said that the live baby was hers.

Solomon said, "Bring me a sword. When they did, he said, "Divide the living child in two and give half to the one, and half to the other."

Then the first woman, who was the true mother, said, "Give her the living child and in no wise slay it. The other woman said, "Let it be neither mine nor thine, but divide it."

King Solomon immediately knew who the true mother was, for a mother would never let her child be hurt, so he gave the baby to the first woman.

All of Israel heard of King Solomon's judgment, and they saw that the wisdom of God was in him.

DISCUSSION QUESTIONS
1. Who became the next king of Israel?
2. What did Solomon ask for when he prayed?
3. Did God give to Solomon what he asked for? Why?
4. What did Solomon do about the two women who each claimed that a baby was hers?

5. Did Solomon make a wise decision?

6. What would you ask to be blessed with if you could have anything? Why?

7. Would your choice be wise in the long run?

RECIPE
1/4 cup sifted flour
2 TBSP. sugar
1 TBSP. cornstarch
Dash of salt
2 TBSP. oil
1 egg white
1 TBSP. water

Prepare numbered discussion questions on strips of paper.

In mixing bowl, sift together dry ingredients. Add oil and egg white, stirring until mixture is smooth. Add water and mix thoroughly. Make one cookie at a time. On lightly greased skillet or griddle, pour 1 TBSP. of the batter and spread to a 3 1/2" circle. Cook over low heat until lightly browned, about 4 minutes. Turn with wide pancake turner and cook 1 minute more. Working quickly, place cookie on pot holder and put question in the center. Fold cookie in half, then fold again over edge of bowl. Place cookies in muffin pan to cool. Makes 8.

After they're made, have your family crack the cookies open and see how "wise" they are in answering the questions.

Raven Snack

God protects those who serve him. When Elijah, a prophet, had to run and hide for his life, God sent ravens to bring him food to eat.

STORY: 1 Kings 16: 29-33, 17. Many years passed, and Ahab became king of Israel. He married a woman named Jezebel. Together, they did many evil things and were very wicked.

Elijah was a righteous man and a prophet. Ahab and Jezebel did not like him because he was good and did not approve of their evil ways. One day, the Lord came to Elijah and told him he needed to go and hide by a brook called Cherith, for Jezebel and Ahab were going to try and kill him.

Elijah did what the Lord told him to do. He drank of the water from the brook, and ravens, sent by the Lord, brought him food to eat. Elijah was protected and taken care of because he obeyed.

DISCUSSION QUESTIONS
1. Who were Ahab and Jezebel?
2. Were they righteous?
3. Why did Elijah have to go and hide?
4. How did he eat?
5. Did God take care of Elijah?

RECIPE
4 cups any granola
1/2 cup peanuts
1/2 cup coconut
1/2 cup dried apples or dried bananas
1/2 cup M&Ms

Mix together all ingredients, and you have a yummy snack that a raven would have put together!

Elijah's Bread Pudding

Elijah was saved again when a famine came and God sent him into a city where he met a widow and her son. The widow showed great faith by using the last of her ingredients to make Elijah some bread to eat. She was well paid for her kindness by the miracles which took place afterwards.

STORY: 1 Kings 17:10-24. Elijah stayed by the brook until it dried up because there hadn't been any rain in the land. The Lord told Elijah to go into a certain city, where he would find a widow who would give him something to eat and drink.

Elijah went into the city and found the widow. He asked her for some water and some bread. She gave him water, but told him that she only had enough ingredients to make a little bread for herself and her son.

Elijah asked the widow to go and make him some bread first, and promised her that if she did so, her flour and oil wouldn't be gone. She would have enough to bake other food, as well.

The woman went and did as Elijah asked, and it was just as Elijah had said. She and her son had enough food for many days.

After a short time, the son of the woman got sick and died. The woman was very upset and got angry with Elijah. But Elijah said to her, "Give me thy son." He carried the boy to his own bed and prayed, then stretched himself on the boy three times, asking the Lord to bring the boy back to life.

The Lord answered Elijah's prayer and brought the boy back to life. When his mother saw that her son lived, she told Elijah that she now knew he was a man of God.

DISCUSSION QUESTIONS
1. Where did Elijah go when the famine came and the brook dried up?
2. How did Elijah help the woman and her son?
3. How did they help him?
4. What were the two great miracles that happened while Elijah stayed with the widow and her son?
5. The widow showed great faith by preparing bread for Elijah with her last bit of flour and oil. Can you think of a time that you showed faith by doing something God asked you to do?

RECIPE
4 eggs
2 cups milk
1/3 cup sugar
1/2 tsp. cinnamon
1/2 tsp. vanilla
1/4 tsp. salt
2 1/2 cups dry bread cubes (3 1/2 slices)
1/2 cup raisins

Beat together eggs, milk, sugar, cinnamon, vanilla, and salt in mixing bowl. Place dry bread cubes in an 8 x 1 1/2" round baking dish. Sprinkle raisins over bread. Pour egg mixture over all. Bake in a 325° oven for 40-45 minutes, or until a knife inserted near the center comes out clean. Cool slightly. Serves 6.

Fantastic Flaming Altar Ring

Elijah helps to demonstrate God's power in this wonderful story of the wicked priests of Baal. You and your family can create your own flaming, delicious altar ring.

STORY: 1 Kings 18:17-37. After Elijah stayed with the widow and her son, the Lord told him to go and see King Ahab. There was a great famine in the land; it hadn't rained for a long time, so there was little food and water. The Lord told Elijah that if he went to see Ahab, he would send rain.

Elijah went and saw Ahab and told him to gather his whole city to Mount Carmel, along with the 450 prophets of Baal. Ahab did as Elijah asked, and when all the people were gathered, he told them they could not follow both God and Baal.

Elijah presented a challenge to the prophets of Baal. He said that they were to each have a sacrifice at an altar, but instead of building a fire as they usually did, he said that the evil priests should call on their god to light the fire, and Elijah would call upon his God.

The priests went first. They called upon their god, chanting and leaping on the altar. At noon, Elijah said that their god must be sleeping and that they needed to wake him up. The priests cried out some more, but no one answered and there was no fire.

Elijah then built an altar and made a trench around it. He then put wood on the altar and said, "Fill four barrels with water and pour it on the sacrifice and on the wood. The people obeyed him and put water on it three times. Water was everywhere on the altar and overfilling the trenches.

Elijah then called upon God, saying, "Lord God of Abraham, Isaac and of Israel, let it be known this day that thou art God in Israel and that I am thy servant and that I have done all these things at thy word."

Just then, God sent a fire that consumed the sacrifice and the wood and the stones, as well as the dust. Not even the water in the trenches was left. When the people saw this miracle, they fell to the ground and said they knew that God had accomplished this miracle.

DISCUSSION QUESTIONS
1. What was the name of the idol the wicked people worshipped?
2. Why was it bad for them to worship Baal?
3. How did Elijah convince the people that God has power, while idols don't?
4. Is there anything in your life that you are worshipping more than God? (Money, material things, power, popularity, etc.)
5. If you've found something that you worship more than God, make a plan for turning yourself around. What will your plan be?

RECIPE
3 packages buttermilk biscuits
1 cup sugar
1/2 cup butter
1 tsp. cinnamon
5 TBSP. milk
8 sugar cubes
Lemon extract

Cut the biscuits in half and place in a greased tube pan. Stir sugar, butter, cinnamon, and milk into saucepan and bring to a boil. Pour mixture over biscuits. Bake at 350° for 35 minutes. Turn out on large plate and surround with sugar cubes which have been soaked in lemon extract. Light cubes. When the flames die down, cut up and eat!

Floating Axe Fondue

Elisha performed a miracle by making an iron axe head float on the water so that the man who borrowed it wouldn't get in trouble. You will use a fork to make marshmallows "float" in the fondue sauce.

STORY: 2 Kings 6:1-7. The sons of the prophets told Elisha that they wanted to go to Jordan and settle there. Elisha agreed and told them to go. One of the men asked Elisha to go with them, and Elisha said that he would.

After they had arrived in Jordan, one day they were cutting down trees for wood. But as one man was chopping, his axe head fell off into the water. The man cried and said to Elisha that he had borrowed the axe.

Elisha asked where it fell into the water, and the man showed him. Elijah then cut down a stick and threw it into the water where the axe head had fallen. Suddenly, the iron axe head floated to the top of the water where the man could reach it.

DISCUSSION QUESTIONS
1. Where did Elisha and the sons of the prophets go?
2. What happened one day when they were chopping down trees?
3. What did Elisha do?
4. Is it possible for a heavy iron axe head to float?
5. Who do you think helped Elisha make the axe head float?
6. Have you ever had an experience when Heavenly Father made the impossible possible?

RECIPE
12 ounces milk chocolate
3/4 cup light cream
2 TBSP. orange juice
Large marshmallows

Melt milk chocolate and cream in saucepan. Remove from heat and stir in orange juice. Pour in fondue pot to keep warm. Place marshmallows on forks and dip into the mixture for a yummy treat!

Jonah's Whale Of A Dessert

Jonah learned that nobody can hide from God or from what they need to do. Even in the depths of the belly of a fish, God knew where Jonah was. Jonah knew he needed to trust God and do what God commanded him to do.

STORY: Jonah 1-3. Jonah was told by God to go to Nineveh, which was a very wicked city. Jonah was afraid to go, so he tried to run away. He got on a ship and tried to run away from God. But God knew where he was, and he sent a great storm which threatened to sink the ship that Jonah was on.

The men on the ship were afraid and went to Jonah, asking him who he was and why this was happening. Jonah told them that God was angry with him, for he had disobeyed, and he told them to throw him into the sea. The men didn't want to do this and they tried to get to the shore, but the wind would not let them. Finally, they took Jonah and threw him into the sea.

God then sent a huge fish to swallow Jonah, and he prayed while he was in the fish's belly. He said how sorry he was to have disobeyed, and he asked to be saved. After three days and nights, the fish spit Jonah out on dry land.

Again, God told Jonah to go to Nineveh. This time, Jonah obeyed and preached there. The people of Nineveh listened to Jonah and believed in God. Jonah learned that God would prepare a way for the things he needed accomplished.

DISCUSSION QUESTIONS
1. Who was Jonah?
2. Why did Jonah run away?
3. Where did he go?
4. When the storm came, what did Jonah tell the men to do to make it stop?
5. After they threw him into the water, what happened to Jonah?
6. How do you think Jonah felt inside that big fish?
7. Can we run away from God if we do something wrong?

RECIPE
1 package (4 serving size) blueberry gelatin
1 cup boiling water
1 cup cold water
1 1/2 cups swedish or gummy fish
1 cup marshmallows, regular or mini
Frozen whipped topping, thawed (if desired)

Pour gelatin into a bowl. Add boiling water to gelatin. Stir with rubber scraper until gelatin is completely dissolved, about 2 minutes. Add cold water. Using measuring cup, scoop gelatin from bowl into 6 clear plastic or glass cups or serving bowls. Put all cups into refrigerator to chill until gelatin is thickened, about 45 minutes. Take cups out of refrigerator and add fish. Stir gently. Put marshmallows on top. Put back into refrigerator to chill until firm, about 2 hours. If desired, top with whipped topping.

Hebrews' Healthy Compote

By obeying God, Daniel, Shadrach, Meshach, and Abednego were healthier and wiser. You can be too, by following the Word of Wisdom! The compote you make has many healthy things in it to enjoy.

STORY: Daniel 1: 1-20. The king of Babylon had a few of the Hebrew children come to live and learn at his house. He gave them a certain portion of his meat and wine to eat.

Among these children were Daniel, Shadrach, Meshach, and Abednego. They asked the man in charge of them if they could have healthful food instead of meat, and water to drink. The man in charge was afraid, for he didn't want the king to be angry with him.

But Daniel asked him to try an experiment. For ten days, he would feed Daniel and his friends good food and drink. At the end of those days, they would be compared to the other children who drank wine and ate the king's meat.

The man in charge agreed. At the end of ten days, the king sent for Daniel and his friends and found that they were ten times better in wisdom and understanding than all of his magicians and astrologers. God had blessed them because they obeyed.

DISCUSSION QUESTIONS
1. What were the names of four of the Jewish children who came to live with the king of Babylon?
2. Why wouldn't Daniel and his friends eat the food and wine the king sent them?
3. What did they want to eat instead?
4. What happened after ten days?
5. How did God bless Daniel, Shadrach, Meshach, and Abednego?
6. Has the Lord given us counsel on what foods we should eat and others we should avoid? Where?
7. Name some foods or drinks that we shouldn't take into our bodies.

RECIPE
1 package (8 oz.) reduced-fat cream cheese, softened
1/2 cup fat-free sour cream

1/2 cup sugar
3 TBSP. almond flavoring
2 TBSP. light whipped topping
1 pint sliced peaches, melon balls, or sliced bananas
1 pint strawberries, raspberries, or blueberries

Beat cream cheese and sour cream in small mixing bowl at medium speed with electric mixer until well blended. Blend in sugar, almond flavoring, and whipped topping. Chill.

Place fruit in individual serving dishes and top with cream cheese sauce. Makes 4-6 servings.

Protecting Angel Cake

By keeping the commandments and going against a law they knew to be wrong, Shadrach, Meshach, and Abednego were protected from the fiery furnace by a heavenly visitor.

STORY: Daniel 3:1-29. King Nebuchadnezzar made a golden idol and set it up for all to worship. He decreed that at the sound of music, all in his kingdom should fall down and worship the idol.

There were three men who would not worship the idol. The king sent for Shadrach, Meshach, and Abednego to come to him when he heard they would not worship as he wished them to. When they came, King Nebuchadnezzar told them that if they did not obey him, they would be thrown into the fiery furnace. But the men said that they would not worship the idol. If they were to be thrown into the furnace, they said they knew that God had the power to save them.

The king was very angry at these words, and commanded that the furnace be made seven times hotter than it usually was. Then he ordered the most mighty men in his army to take the righteous men and throw them in the furnace.

The fire from the furnace was so hot that it immediately killed those who threw Shadrach, Meshach, and Abednego into it. The king then looked inside the furnace to make sure the men were killed; but instead, he saw four men walking around in the fire! They were Shadrach, Meshach, Abednego, and a protecting angel.

The king knew that what he was seeing was miraculous, and he called to Shadrach, Meshach, and Abednego to come out. When they left the furnace, the king and those around him saw that the men were safe. Not a hair on their heads had been singed, and they didn't even smell like smoke.

The king then made a decree that nobody could speak badly about the God of Shadrach, Meshach, and Abednego, for he knew that there was no other God who could perform this sort of miracle.

DISCUSSION QUESTIONS
1. What did the king of Babylon build?
2. What did he order people to do to the golden idol?
3. What did Shadrach, Meshach, and Abednego do?
4. What did the king do when he heard about their refusal to worship his idol?
5. Did the fire kill them? Why not?
6. When they came out, what law did the king make?
7. Are there idols in these days that the world tries to make us worship? (Examples: money, power, movie stars, material things, etc.)
8. Take a good look at your life. Are you worshipping God or one of these idols? How can you do better?

RECIPE
1 package yellow or white cake mix
1 1/2 cups water
2 eggs
1 package (7 1/2 oz.) fluffy white frosting mix
1 cup water
2 sugar cubes
10 chocolate chips
1 tsp. lemon extract

Generously grease and flour a 13x9" baking pan. Prepare the cake mix as directed on the package. (When you break the eggs, crack each in the middle and pour out the egg. Then save the 2 best shell halves. Wash these halves and turn upside down to dry.) After mixing, pour the batter into the pan.

Bake in 350° oven 35-40 minutes or until wooden pick inserted in the center comes out clean. Cool the cake 10 minutes on rack, then remove from pan to tray. After the cake is cool, measure across one short edge of the cake and mark the center with a wooden pick. Measure 2 and 4 inches down each long edge and mark with picks. Prepare the frosting as directed on package.

Cut the cake between the center wooden pick and side picks in a curve to make a rounded top for the angel's head. Slide the cut corners down the sides to about the center of the cake. Turn the corners so the cut sides are up, to make arms that look as if they're reaching out. Attach the arms to the sides of the cake with some of the frosting, using spatula. Frost the cake with the spatula. Place the 2 egg shell halves, round sides down, on the top of the "arms" as hands. Place 1 sugar cube in each shell half. Make a smiling mouth of chocolate chips and eyes with 2 chocolate chips.

Just before serving, pour 1/2 tsp. lemon extract over each sugar cube. Light and enjoy!

Daniel's Loyal Lions

Because of the jealousy of some wicked men, Daniel was thrown into the lions' den. With Heavenly Father on his side, Daniel knew that he would be protected, even from the hungry lions.

STORY: Daniel 6: 1-27. When King Darius became the new king of Babylon, he chose three presidents to help him. The first was a man named Daniel. King Darius liked Daniel and wanted to make him a leader over all the other leaders.

The others who worked for King Darius were jealous of Daniel and plotted to have him killed. They told King Darius that he should make a law saying that no one could pray for thirty days, and if they did, they would be thrown into the lions' den. King Darius agreed, and the law was signed.

Daniel heard the law, but he still prayed to God three times a day. The evil men caught him and brought him before King Darius. King Darius didn't want to put Daniel in the lions' den, but he had signed a law and had no choice.

Before Daniel was put into the lions' den, the king said that he believed that Daniel's God would save him. Daniel was put in with the lions, and a huge stone covered the doorway.

The king fasted all night for Daniel, and in the morning he went to the lions' den. He said, "O Daniel, servant of the living God, is thy God, whom thou servest continually, able to deliver thee from the lions?" Daniel answered him, saying that God had sent an angel who shut the lions' mouths, and he was not hurt.

Daniel was released, and the king commanded that those men who had accused

Daniel and plotted against him should be thrown into the lions' den themselves.

King Darius then made a decree that all men should know that the God of Daniel was the living God.

DISCUSSION QUESTIONS
1. Who was Daniel?
2. Did the other men Daniel worked with like him?
3. What did they do to try and get rid of Daniel?
4. Did Daniel stop praying to God when he heard the law? Why not?
5. What happened to Daniel in the lions' den?
6. Do you think we should obey God no matter what? Did Daniel?

RECIPE
1 package (4-serving size) lemon gelatin
1 cup boiling water
1 cup cold water
Coconut
Jelly beans
Mandarin oranges
4 chocolate chips

Pour gelatin into a bowl. Add boiling water to gelatin. Stir until dissolved, about 2 minutes. Add cold water. Stir. Scoop gelatin into dessert dishes almost to the top. Put dishes into refrigerator to chill until firm, about 3 hours. Let each family member decorate their own "lion face" with coconut for the mane, mandarin oranges for the ears and mouth (2 of them coming down from the chocolate chip nose) and 2 jelly beans for the eyes.

Esther's Shocking Pink Fruit Feast

Esther showed her courage and faithfulness in this story. In the end at the feast, Esther revealed the wicked plans of a wicked man and saved her people from death.

STORY: Esther 1-8. The king of Babylon gave a big feast and invited many people to come. He showed them many of his riches, then sent for the queen, for he wanted to show everyone how beautiful she was. But the queen refused. The king was angry that she had not obeyed him, and he wanted to choose a new queen.

Many of the king's officers went around the kingdom and gathered the most beautiful maidens so the king could choose his new wife. Among them was a beautiful Jewish girl named Esther, whose uncle was named Mordecai.

When Esther arrived, the king favored her over the others, though he didn't know that Esther was a Jew. The king made her his queen.

Haman was one of the king's leaders. He made the people bow down to him when they saw him. But Mordecai, who was a Jew, would not bow down to him. Haman was angry at him and at all the Jews, so he told the king that the Jews wouldn't obey the king's laws. He also advised the king that they must kill all the Jews since they wouldn't obey the laws.

Letters were sent out to the leaders in the kingdom, ordering that every Jew should be killed. When the Jews heard about the letters, they began to weep, then they fasted and prayed for help.

When Queen Esther heard about the letters, she was very upset and sent for Mordecai to tell her why this was happening. Mordecai told Esther that she would be killed along with the other Jews, and that she needed to try and save her people. Esther asked all the Jews to fast with her for three days. At the end of that time, she went to the king. In those days, if anyone came to the king without being asked to come, they were put to death. But Esther gathered her courage and went anyway.

The king was not angry with Esther for coming, and he told her that she could have anything she wanted. Esther asked that the king and Haman might come to a feast. The king agreed.

When Haman and the king came to the feast, Esther told the king about Haman's plan to kill the Jews and that she was a Jew. The king was very angry at Haman's deviousness, and had him killed. He then put a stop to the killings by having Mordecai write letters to all the kingdom. Mordecai then told the people that they could kill anyone who tried to kill them.

Queen Esther had saved her people, and the Jews celebrated their deliverance.

DISCUSSION QUESTIONS
1. Why did the king decide to pick a new queen?
2. Who did he pick?
3. Why did Haman wish to have all the Jews killed?
4. What did Queen Esther do to save the Jews?
5. What did the king do to Haman?
6. Esther showed great courage by going to the king when those who came without a summons were put to death. Can you think of a time that you or someone in your family showed great courage?

RECIPE
1 container (8 oz.) soft cream cheese
1 package (4 serving size) gelatin, any red flavor
1/4 cup milk
Fruit for dipping: Apples, bananas, oranges, etc.

Add gelatin and milk to cream cheese in a small bowl. Beat with wire whisk until well blended and smooth. Put mixture into serving bowl and chill in refrigerator until serving time. When ready to serve, let dip stand at room temperature to soften slightly, if necessary (about 15 minutes). Place bowl on large plate. Arrange fruit on plate around bowl at serving time. Makes about 1 1/2 cups of dip.

Job's Popcorn Jewel Cake

Job was put through many trials and lost all he had, but he did not blame God or stop loving him. Because he stayed so faithful through it all, God blessed him with even more than he had before. Job is like the popcorn in this cake, which starts out as a little seed, hardly anything at all, but after it's heated and gone through trials, it is twice as big as it was! It's blessed with gumdrop "jewels" and marshmallow richness.

STORY: Job 1-42. Job was a very righteous man who obeyed God. He was also very blessed, for he had a wife and ten children and many animals and servants. God knew that Job was righteous.

Satan said that Job was righteous only because he was rich and had been given so much. God told Satan that he could take everything away from Job, but he couldn't hurt him. In doing so, he would see that Job was righteous.

After that, things got very bad for Job. All of his oxen and servants were killed, and a fire burned all his sheep. Besides this, all of his camels were stolen. Worst of all, a strong wind blew down Job's son's house, and all of Job's children were killed. Job had nothing left.

Even though Job was very sad, he wasn't angry at God. He said that when he was born he had nothing, and then God had given him everything. Now, God had let it be taken away. He fell down and worshipped God, for he still loved him.

God told Satan that Job had been righteous, even when everything had been taken from him. But Satan said that Job wouldn't be righteous if he was very sick. God told Satan that he could make Job sick, but he couldn't kill him.

So Job became very sick. His body was covered with sores that were so bad, he wished he had never been born. Job's wife asked Job if he still thought that God was good. Job said that God gave people good things, and sometimes he let bad things happen. But it wasn't because the people were bad, for sometimes bad things happen to good people.

Three of Job's friends came to see him, and they told him that God punishes wicked people. So, they figured, Job must have done something wicked.

Job told his friends to go away, for they weren't helping him. He loved God and said that he had not been wicked. He might die, but he knew that if he did, he would be resurrected and see God.

His friends told Job again to repent, then God would help him get well. Job said he had been righteous and that God knew it. Sometimes, he said, wicked people have no trouble and righteous people have many troubles.

Then Job heard God's voice asking him many questions. Job said that he did not understand all things. God told him that men do not always understand God, but that they need to trust in him. Then Job was privileged to see God.

God told Job's friends that he was angry with them for telling Job things that were not true. Job prayed for his friends as they burned sacrifices.

After all of his trials, God blessed Job with even more than he had before. He and his wife had more children and more animals. Job lived to be a very old and righteous man.

DISCUSSION QUESTIONS
1. Who was Job?
2. What bad things happened to him?
3. Was he angry at God for letting those things happen to him?
4. What did Job's friends tell Job to do? Why?
5. Was that right? Why?
6. Job was very faithful and loved God, even though so many bad things had happened to him. Do you think you could be that strong and faithful if so many bad things happened to you?
7. How can we strengthen our faith in and love for God?
8. Are you going to let trials and problems drag you down, or are you going to learn and grow stronger from them as Job did?

RECIPE
Let your family examine the popcorn kernels before you pop them. They don't seem like much, do they? But when added to heat, or like Job, trials, they end up being twice as big as they were.

2 quarts popped popcorn
3/4 cup peanuts
1 cup gumdrops

2 TBSP. butter
2 cups marshmallows

Butter a 13x9" glass baking dish. Mix popcorn, peanuts, and gumdrops together in a large pan. Melt butter and marshmallows together over low heat until butter and marshmallows are melted. Pour over popcorn mixture. Mix well. When popcorn is thoroughly coated, pour into buttered dish. Refrigerate. Cut when cool. Makes 24 pieces.